WAYS THINGS MOVE

by Robin Nelson

first step nonfiction

Lerner

Lerner Books • London • New York • Minneapolis

A **force** is a push or a pull.

Forces make things move in different ways.

Children walk in a
straight line.

A train moves in a straight line.

A crayon draws a
zigzag line.

Skiers make zigzag paths in the snow.

A hoop spins in a **circle.**

A wheel moves in a circle.

A swing moves
backwards and forwards.

A rocking chair moves
backwards and forwards.

A toy car can move quickly.

A bike can move quickly.

A toy boat can move slowly.

A heavy box is pushed slowly.

Everything moves with a push.

Everything moves with a pull.

The Zigzag Street

There is a zigzag street in San Francisco, California, USA. Some people call it the crooked street. The street goes down a very steep hill. The street was made with many short, sharp turns all the way to the bottom of the hill. The street was made like this so that cars would not go down the hill too fast.

Moving Facts

 A guitar string moves backwards and forwards very rapidly when you pluck it. The string is vibrating. Vibrate means to move backwards and forwards rapidly.

 A cheetah can run faster than any other animal on land.

 A snail is one of the slowest animals on land.

Racing cars are driven on a track that is like a circle. In some races, the cars are driven around the track about 200 times!

 Some animals run in a zigzag pattern to escape danger. Rabbits and deer run left and right to confuse whatever is chasing them. This also makes it hard to follow them.

Glossary

 circle – a round shape

 force – a push or a pull

 straight – no turns or curves

 zigzag – a line that goes one way then turns another way

Index

The photographs in this book are reproduced through the courtesy of: Digital Vision Royalty Free, cover, pp. 8, 12, 22 (top); © John Henley/CORBIS, p. 2; © Diane Meyer, p. 3; © Kwame Saikomo/ SuperStock, pp. 4, 22 (second from bottom); © Chris Fairclough, p. 5; © Todd Strand/Independent Picture Service, pp. 6, 15, 22 (second from top and bottom); Corbis Royalty Free, pp. 7, 13; Minneapolis Public Library, p. 9; Stockbyte Royalty Free, p. 10; © Ariel Skelley/CORBIS, p. 11; © Jane Sapinsky/CORBIS, p. 14; Brand X Pictures, p. 16; © Photodisc Royalty Free by Getty Images, p. 17; © Ron Watts/CORBIS, p. 18.

This book was first published in the United States of America in 2004.

First published in the United Kingdom in 2008 by
Lerner Books,
Dalton House,
60 Windsor Avenue,
London SW19 2RR

Website address: www.lernerbooks.co.uk

This edition was updated and edited for UK publication by Discovery Books Ltd., Unit 3, 37 Watling Street, Leintwardine, Shropshire SY7 0LW

Words in **bold** are explained in the glossary on page 22.

British Library Cataloguing in Publication Data

Nelson, Robin, 1971-
Way things move. - (First step nonfiction. Forces)
1. Motion - Juvenile literature
I. Title
531

ISBN-13: 978 1 58013 370 8

Printed in China